MUSE

A COLLECTION OF SIMPLE POEMS

Sruthi Dhulipala

BookLeaf
Publishing

India | USA | UK

Presentation by *BookLeaf Publishing*

Web: www.bookleafpub.com

E-mail: info@bookleafpub.com

ISBN: 9789358738988

First edition 2021

ACKNOWLEDGEMENTS

Firstly, I'd love to thank my family and friends who have been my muse for this "Muse." This book consists of poems that I've lived and experienced and I'd like to acknowledge my near and dear who taught me life lessons, who gave me precious moments to cherish, and who stood by my side while I pursued my artistic dreams.

I would also like to thank Book Leaf Publishing for pushing writers and poets such as myself to publishing an anthology and for believing in my work.

"Muse" came out of personal experiences and sceneries I envisioned and embraced, and beauty of little things around me. And it also came from music and my love to compose tunes. So, I am also extremely grateful for the art around me that motivated me constantly while I wrote the poems in this book.

DEDICATIONS

To my family, Kavita, Murthy, and Pranav

To my first muse

To music

To love and

To loss

1. MY SERAPH

From the womb that felt safe and sound,

To the arms of a nurse, I was passed around.

Sounds around me, faint mutters of delight,

Coos and kisses, some soft, few rasping.

With a stutter of eyelids, I attempted to look into the light,

A blurred haze, as I toiled to perceive the power of sight.

My first sound- a cry, a soft shriek from inside,

Gazes locked on me, while I looked back with my eyes wide.

But when passed on to her, I gaped, such elation enfolded,

Warmth in her eyes, with tender hums, she gently caressed.

To her, I was an angel from the sky, who had just taken birth,

And to me, she was the angel for she brought me to earth.

Time galloped and soon I was a toddler,

My hurdle rested forward, the intent to amble.

She helped me, trot by trot, holding my hand as I walked.

I looked at her with unconditional affection when she talked.

Her gazes, they held concern airing her tender face,

Her nurture, so unembellished and with her, life is such a beautiful place.

Soon, came my first day at school and yes, I cried.

Wailing and weeping, not letting her leave my side.

She calmed me, promising she would be waiting right outside

And she stood there, when I returned, wearing a gleam of pride

Seeing her, I ran into her arms, eyes rolling off a tear.

She hugged me and in a flash, dissipated my fear.

When I blew my nose, when I caught a flu,

When I tripped down and when I needed looking to,

She aided me, and helped me set everything right.

She stayed up all night, concern endearing,

In no time, I grew up, from a kid to a teen

Ready to risk, to unravel the world unseen.

Moods turn in a rapid rush, the energy all in me

The desire to prove myself and the urge for the world to see

Though she warned me of bad things, I did not heed

Made mistakes, and she helped me when in need.

She battled life for me, taught me to be unrelenting

I admire her, for that poise never dwindling.

Years passed and turned me mature and wise.

Off I leave to college, to move on, to make my own choice

As I look back, memories in an idyll,

Yesterday, I was striving to walk and today I began to fly.

She made it all possible, I am strong, she said.

When I fell, she held me so my wings don't shred

She made me ready, to fasten and to take off,

To soar high, to step up into the world, a big step

Believe me; I am scared, for what's outside is unknown

But, with her by my side, I know I would not be alone.

As I walk away from my house, I bear a smile, curved wide

With the strength that I have gained and a tint of pride

Today, when asked who taught me to be strong

I say, it's because my mother, she raised me that way.

2. INTO A BOOK

A cup of coffee and a comforting couch.

That, to me, is my antiserum for the monotonous day.

I cup my hands around the warm mug,

And open the book that waited for me all day.

I cupped my hands across the mug with my icy fingers,

And behind my glasses, I started to read.

My eyebrows started to pucker, as I thumbed the ivory pages over.

The story pulled and transported me into a land unknown,

The world began to fade into a blurry haze.

As the narrator kept at his storyteller's pace.

Joy, disdain, and many other emotions encircled in the air.

The hero's charm so lifelike, or is it a mark of pretense?

As the pages flipped, my heart thumped away inchmeal,

Emotions plastered all over my rapt face.

Love aired the story, the characters seemed to care.

Delight and laughter all around, oh, this is turning out so well.

But, wait! Why do I sense something odd?

I move along to see the story sway.

All of a sudden, I envision a betrayal.

My mind begins to shout, "this is not right."

I try to reach out to the characters, but in vain.

I could only see the turmoil be caused anyway is ghastly pain.

I gasped at the twist as I got pulled down along with the girl with the rationale.

She felt abhorrent and so did I, for I was her in the story line.

The flipping became harder and the pages turned quicker.

At every stage, I felt the excitement of a better way.

The pages started to thin and with it, my patience.

I wanted answers, I wanted them right away.

I did not want to experience the end yet,

But there seemed no other way out.

Oh, the story ended and all was well again.

But, It took me a few moments to wander back in

To leave an alternate world and hit reality

Back to my cozy couch, I look up and found myself smiling

This was an adventure and I was one within their world

That's the thing about books, they take you far and wide.

Sway you and leave you in the monotony again.

The mystery - it unfolds you, at every single stride.

Yet, we love them and cannot stop taking another ride.

Another dreary day, but I did not feel the strain.

Revitalized, I felt a sense of calm as I closed the book

And went back into the monotony again.

3. GROWING UP

All throughout your life

You had a hand by your side.

Guiding you

Telling you what's right.

Slowly, the hand starts to loosen

Wiggles as you hold it tighter.

Slipping away like chalky sand

From your frazzled clasp.

Before you know it

You're set loose.

Hurled into slippery ice

Stumbling to find your foot.

Slowly you regain balance

Totter around in this bleak unknown.

Figure your moves prudently

And twirl around on your own.

Somehow, you like it

You feel alright.

Yes, you fell face first

But you picked up alright.

Growing up, that's what you did

You felt pain at first

You even feared life.

But then prosperity came

And, all was okay.

Cherish growing up

For this is your time to explore

Before you come back

Looking for that hand

To grip, yet again.

4. FROSTY NIGHT

A quiet night, cold and wintry

Clouds concealing the hazy moonlight

A faint sound of crickets in harmony

And an eerily romantic vibe.

I nuzzle into a giant fleece sweater

Pressing my palms into the warm sleeves

Squatting by the brick fireplace, I sighed

Sniffing the fire that smelled like burnt s'mores.

Smiling at the crackling fire,

I let my mind wander away.

I dreamt of this moment once

When I was eight years old

While reading an Enid Blyton novel

And imagined myself in the book.

I dreamt of walking in the snow

And sipping hot cocoa indoors

I dreamt of rustic fireplaces

And cozy experiences of a frosty night.

The dream manifested itself today

And it's so much better than what I imagined

It made me happy, this moment

Something I'd write in my diary to remember again.

Smiling at the crackling fire,

Into a peaceful night's sleep, I doze away.

5. MY BEST MAN

Sitting under a mango tree to sulk,

I waited for you to come find your little girl.

Pat me on my tiny shoulder,

And say, dear child - it's alright.

Clutching my little finger,

And tugging me home, a step at a time.

You were my pal and I your dear little pet.

Us versus the world, living every moment.

Today you're slipping away, and I'm scared.

I'm not ready to lose you just yet.

If not you, who would take me around?

Who would make me feel safe and sound?

If not for you, I wouldn't have come this far.

Yet you still look at me, like I'm always small.

I'm lost now, like a shell in a sea,

But here I hold together,

Hope still with me.

I close my eyes to the happy times,

To our stories over tea,

To the times when you told me,

To be bold and carefree.

Now, it's my time to tell you,

Be strong and fight for me.

This little girl still needs her grandpa,

So, please stay with me.

You flutter your eyelids,

And I jump to stand your side.

Fluffing the pillow below your head, holding your hand,

Weakly looking around, you strain a faint smile.

I sighed loud in the moment,

You stayed strong, you fought for me.

It'll be okay, it should be.

I'm not ready to lose you yet,

For, without you, I'm only a lost shell in the sea.

6. ZEN IN WAVES

One gloomy evening, I wandered out,

Down the road, across a muddy trail, to the beach.

Greeted by the salt in the air and a musky whiff,

The waves hushing in a four-count swing beat.

I let out a deep sigh, smiling at what lay ahead,

This is my happy place, and it always will be.

I dug my feet into the warm sand,

Watched the seagulls trot away in pride.

A ship set sail and I watched it drift away.

Sketching rings of freedom behind its mighty glides.

The waves now turned to subdues hushes, like a mother's whisper.

I stepped forth, to feel the cold waters touch my feet,

The sand beneath slipping away in gentle drift.

As I bent down to touch it, to feel its pure minutiae,

Watch it escape within my fingers and greet the approaching wave.

The wiggle sought to my intimate thoughts

Tickled my skin into substantial serenity.

A woman with words,

I still stunned into silence.

Gazing at the hue in the Adam's Ale

With greens that mimicked the mighty panorama

Came here to quench my thirst,

Not of the body, but of the soul.

The sea, it sang to me, a harmonious melody.

It filled my heart, with tranquil,

Bliss in its little joys, like a walk to the beach.

7. A WRITER

I write a poem,

I scribble a song,

I mumble a rant that's endless,

And sometimes, squiggle them all.

Once I describe a blue jay in a saintly ode,

And once, it's about the light at the end of the road.

Sometimes, it's my innermost revelations,

And at times, a mindless rant about fluster and distress.

But in the end, it's the heart that talks.

Wanting to express what's within.

Either with words that rhyme,

Or with a book with plots and diegesis.

The same heart that yearns for a fairy tale,

That flutters in delight at the sight of love.

That melts away at a silken voice,

The same heart that shows you how to love.

I am a woman of words; I write.

To show you the vastness of emotions,

Buried in my heart and mind.

I write for my soul,

And for you, to know me more.

8. SHE

She is a lullaby,

Pure and affectionate.

Sending a sense of calm,

Caressing you with kisses and joy.

She is a wave on the beach,

Serene but fiery.

Sweeping you off your feet,

Yet holding her ground in what she believes.

She is a peony,

Compassionate and kind.

Loving you without terms and bounds,

With petals of wisdom that she bore.

She is a thunderstorm,

Angry and determined.

Pouring down waves of emotion,

Yet hiding her truth in the surface beneath.

She is a raindrop,

Delicate and icy.

Plops into your world with a smile,

Washing away any sadness you felt.

She is a survivor,

Living an inspiring life.

Knowing how to forgive and knowing how to heal,

She is strong and all things right.

9. DILEMMA

Two choices. One familiar, one unsung.

Which one to choose?

One promises the comforts I deserve.

And one rewards the happiness I crave.

I squint hard to sneak a peek into both,

To see what lay beyond the mustard clod.

My feet. They dig deeper into the ground,

Frightened and queasy to trudge forward.

Storms hailed and sunny noons soared above,

Yet I stand at rest. Uncertain. Undecided.

How does one choose to sacrifice? How do we let go?

How do we live with the emotions that follow us forevermore?

Tell me, traveler, how are you ever sure?

Do you wait for a miracle to pull you into a path that's meant?

Or, do you push with all your might, to take the first step?

Winter came and frost hit the ground,

Yet I stand at rest. Uncertain. Undecided.

Two choices. One familiar, one unsung.

I am not ready to choose. But one day, I would.

10. MISFITS

You and I, we're misfits in a crowd.

Wandering around to find where we belong.

Turmoil in our minds and dubiety in our hearts,

We nuzzle deeper to stay unnoticed.

In a crowd full of doers, we are dreamers,

Donning our cloaks of invisibility.

We cast a spell to transport us,

Into the nether world far far away.

You and I, we're misfits in a crowd.

Wandering around to find where we belong.

Holding our ground, we frantically find our puzzle,

Lost in our own fantasies, we ignore the crude reality.

Quick in judgments, quick to run away,

To us, all that matters is what's within.

We're odd, abnormal, and most times not understood.

But we belong somewhere, someplace.

Maybe in an island made for misfits.

Who chase stars and live in alternate realms.

Maybe where we're crowned king and queen of an odd bunch.

You and I, we're misfits in a crowd.

Wandering on and on, until we find the place where we truly belong.

11. PAUSE

Hold on, let's hit pause,

At this moment, at this place.

At this fact that we're together again.

I whispered a spell that binds the time to now,

Or so I imagined, to keep myself from worrying away.

Breathing this in, I needed to remember,

I can't let this fade away.

Time's fickle, and so is life,

We chase it by the trails as it gallops away.

With illusions of the memories, we treasure,

Lusting after the ones that we want to visit again.

Wait, I want to hit pause.

I want to breathe this in without thought.

Remember what it feels like to be happy,

With nary a care of tomorrow's wrath.

Can the world wait while we savor this minute?

Can we be greedy and wish for infinity?

Can we live only in hope and happiness?

And a castle that we build from a pipe dream.

If only we could hit pause,

If only we knew how to savor the present,

My heart aches that the minute's ending,

As I let go, hoping to meet this moment again.

12. HEAD OR HEART

But Maa, I love him,

She mumbled quietly.

As she wiped the tears that trickled down,

Wading down her frigid cheeks.

She met a guy, sincere and kind,

Who loved cliche and spoke cars.

Lived in grand gestures and little joys,

And he loved her with all her flaws.

Slowly she fell, for the charm that pure,

He was nice to her, and that's all she saw.

Tried hard to keep her head on the ground,

But her heart swept in the clouds.

She knew it's a lost cause,

For, her mother will never like him at all.

Her heart sunk at reality.

Yet her faith stood high ground.

But Maa, I love him,

She mumbled quietly, yet again.

As she tried to explain,

How safe she felt in his presence.

Spiraling down in inner turmoil,

She struggled to take a call.

Stuck in a crossroads, between life and love,

She wanted a way out.

But Maa, I love him.

She mumbled quietly, one last time with hope in her heart.

Choices are blessings, they said,

But, was this a fair say at all?

13. O' LOST LOVE

O' Lost Love,

If we waited, life could have been different.

Kinder, calmer, happier.

If we fought, dreams could have come true,

Joy, little moments, and twee treasures.

Our time was tested and so was the love,

But we were not prepared for one thing.

The will of the god above.

We never lived in what-could-haves,

Or what might-have-beens.

We only dreamt about the in-betweens.

We pictured a life so pretty,

Glittered it with sparkles and fantasies.

And did not worry about the nitty-gritty.

Maybe it was good we didn't worry,

Maybe it was meant to be that way.

Because somewhere in the naiveté,

We left fears and troubles far away.

O' Lost Love,

If we waited, life could have been different.

But life does not work that way.

Maybe if we fought, we'd be together,

But, life despises any strategic play.

Today I wake up, not with regret,

But with a sense of admiration.

On how we learned life's best truths,

While crafting new stories in our little lives.

O' Lost Love,

If we waited, life could have been different.

But no more wait, no more qualms.

Not for a what-could-have-been, or a what-might-have,

You taught me life, and that I will always cherish,

But now it's time for us to wander off our ways.

In unplanned pathways, but to live our own fates.

14. TRAUMA

Trauma.

Withering a fragile heart that trusted easy.

That turned her into a soul of pain.

Ambushing a tired soul at the hush of the night.

Turning her smiles to anguished frowns.

Truma; it's real even if you say it's not.

Trauma.

When a little was bullied and insulted.

When she knew she was cheated.

When the person you cared about took advantage of you.

When you feel lost and lose the vital moments too.

Truma; it's real even if you say it's not.

Trauma.

It's what you and I face but just don't let the world see.

It's a hollow chest that you drag aimlessly.

Looking for constant care and support.

Fighting to make your heart whole again.

Trauma, it gurgles within and tears you away.

15. SOCIAL STYLES

A bustling feed of shiny lives,

Fake smiles, glitter, and happiness.

I scroll down aimlessly,

Not knowing what I want.

Old friends getting married,

Smiling all rosy-cheeked, happy and alive.

Rita getting her dream job,

Finding her place, this is her time.

I scroll down even further,

A couple at 59, travelling across the world.

Leaving worries in a tightly shut drawer.

Ow, my elbow cramps up and I twist and turn,

Shuffle to another side and continue the journey of the thumbs.

Sunsets, dawn skies, beaches, and starry nights,

I see them all through the glass of my digital matte window.

All of a sudden, I am tired.

A feeling of grief washes over me.

Why ain't I out there? Experiencing these moments for myself?

Fear of missing out on the race that I made up in my mind.

Unaware that I was digging into the Instagram quicksand,

I noticed the sadness was indeed fear of something that never was.

Comparing with the lives of many, wanting too much from life.

Crutching on to reality, I shut the endless app.

And snuggle into a simple dreamless night.

16. MS. SCARLET

She wiped off her fuchsia lipstick

And donned a scarlet bright.

No more coercion.

No more being told what's right.

Her cappuccino skin gleaming,

With the cherry red smile.

She is now a beauty,

But of her own choice.

Her veins spuming with passion,

She is not the norm.

She is fierce and frank,

Ready to evolve into a form.

From here on,

To lead life on her terms.

Unwavering at life's turns,

She left duality at shore.

She is Ms. Scarlett, valorous and blazing

Her newfound beauty, o' a sight to behold

17. SING A SONG

Humming a tune etched into the heart

Caressing the beloved moments from afar.

I sing a song of the soul,

That speaks who I am.

I scribble verses on and on,

Piecing notes and chords all day long.

I sing a song of the soul,

That says what I want.

Flying to places unseen,

Soaring in the imagination within.

I sing a song of the soul,

That lives an adventure every day.

Embracing the feelings scorned,

Finding passion and moving forward.

I sing a song of the soul,

That embraces this fairytale.

18. CALIFORNIAN SUMMER

Golden specks across the fiery red bridge,

Standing where the land ends and the ocean begins.

Breathing in a warm Californian summer,

Sultry and scarlet, sanguinely brilliant.

Lost in time and thought,

Of memories made and people I've met.

Of the time that passed,

And, how happy I felt.

I wonder, are you looking at the sun too?

Are we sharing this moment somehow?

The love for sunsets oceans apart,

I wonder if the skies also have your heart.

Lost in the view, ce magnifique,

I wish I could hit pause.

Sunsets, they make me ponder deep thoughts,

Of many things, small and gargantuan.

Breathing in the warm Californian summer,

Sultry and scarlet, sanguinely brilliant.

I breathe in and let go of the wavering thoughts,

And soak in the drowning sun one last time before it got dark.

19. ONE DAY

All your life, you wait for one day,

The day when you receive what you desire.

When your earnest goals come to life.

And your diligent efforts see the light.

And the day will come, trust the time.

When your soul speaks of all the things you did right.

Sure, people said you can't shine.

They even said you can't get on the other side.

Sure, you got scared and dismal.

But what matters is you hustled till the end.

And the day will come, trust the path.

When all you work for takes shape into life.

Sure, you were confused at times,

You even picked a wrong choice.

But they all came to you as a blessing.

Soon, you will know why.

And the day will come, just trust your choice.

When you look back with a relieved smile.

One day, it will make sense.

One day, you will shine.

20. COME HOME

I come home today,

From the hard-pressed hurdles,

And turbulent tides.

I come home today,

To a safe space,

And comforting arms.

I come home from a year of unraveling,

Voices within, singing umpteen tunes.

Shrugging them aside, I listen,

To the tiny whisper that asks me to go home again.

I come home after a decade,

Not much changed but it also didn't feel the same.

Maybe I grew up, maybe I had too much pain,

But few days in this place,

And the anguish washed away.

I come home,

After wrangling inner demons.

And chasing endless pies in the sky.

I come home,

To a safer morrow.

I come home,

To the place that's mine.